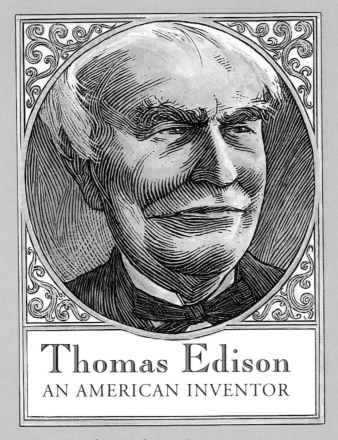

Thomas Edison
AN AMERICAN INVENTOR

by Barbara Gannett

illustrated by Lars Leetaru

Scott Foresma

Editorial Offices: Glenview, Illinois • N
Sales Offices: Reading, Massachusetts • Duluth, Georgia
Glenview, Illinois • Carrollton, Texas • Menlo Park, California

D0003287

Look around you. How many lights do you see? Is there a telephone in the room? a tape recorder? a microphone? a camera?

One man had a lot to do with all these inventions. His name was Thomas Alva Edison.

Thomas Edison was born in 1847. Little Tom started asking questions almost as soon as he could talk. When his family got tired of answering, he figured out another way to learn. He did experiments!

Even as a very little boy, Tom liked to experiment. Once he curled up next to goose eggs. He tried to keep them warm. He wanted to see if he could make them hatch.

Sometimes Tom's experiments got him into trouble. He loved watching everything that went on in the canals near his house. But now and then he got too close and fell in.

Once he lit a small fire. He wanted to watch how it burned. Unfortunately, it got out of control. His dad's barn burned down.

Edison never spent much time
in school.

First he got sick. For a long while, he
was too weak for school. He probably had
scarlet fever.

By the time he was eight, he was well
enough to go to school. But he had lost
some of his hearing when he was sick.
So he didn't do well.

In those days, students had to learn
everything by listening and memorizing.
Tom couldn't hear well enough to be good
at listening.

Tom's teachers thought he couldn't learn. Fortunately, Tom's mother knew how smart he was. She knew he learned best by asking questions and doing experiments. She took him out of school. She taught him herself. He studied every day, all year long. Tom didn't mind. He loved to learn his way!

Tom loved science. He was fascinated with electricity and chemistry. Every penny he earned went into equipment for his experiments.

He worked in a garden and sold the food he grew. He sold candy and newspapers on trains. Then he used his money to buy chemicals and wires.

Tom set up a telegraph experiment with a friend. They strung wire between their houses. Then they sent messages back and forth using Morse code.

Tom got faster and faster at sending and receiving messages. Soon he got a job as a telegrapher. He earned more money, but he didn't spend much of it on clothes or food. Sometimes he didn't even have a place to live. Instead, he bought books and supplies for his experiments.

By this time, Edison knew he wanted to be an inventor. He was sure he could invent a better telegraph machine.

Back then, telegraphs could only send one message at a time. Edison had a theory. He was sure a machine could send four messages at once. To work on this invention, he needed time, money, and a space to work.

Edison was a lucky man. He was visiting a company when some equipment broke. No one could fix it. But Edison saw the problem. He got the machine working again. The owner of the company offered Edison a job.

The job ended a few months later when the company was sold. Still, it gave him the start he needed. Soon he was able to work on lots of inventions at once.

One of the first things Edison worked on was the telephone. The telephone had already been invented. It didn't work well, though. Edison thought he could make it better.

This was not easy, but Thomas Edison never gave up. Finally, after thousands of experiments, he made a better phone.

His work with the telephone gave him
another idea. He had a theory that he could use
a machine to capture sound. People laughed at
this wild idea. No one else thought it could
be done.

Edison worked and worked at it. At last he
came up with the first record player. It recorded
sound on a tube covered with tin foil.

Edison became famous around the world.

Edison's next project was to make a light
that worked using electricity. People had been
trying to invent an electric light for fifty years.
Edison worked on theory after theory. At last
he figured out how to make a light bulb glow
for a long time.

Edison not only invented a long-burning light bulb, but also figured out how to build an electric generator. He also set up wires to carry the electricity into houses.

He set up electric lights for a New Year's Eve party. People were amazed. They had never seen such a strong, steady light at night before.

Life wasn't always easy for Thomas Edison. He became hard of hearing at a young age. He never was good with money. He had a temper. And sometimes he got into trouble.

Still, Thomas Alva Edison became one of America's most brilliant inventors. Edison wasn't afraid to fail. He wasn't afraid to try again and again. He believed that problems could always be solved by thinking and by doing. And he never gave up.